To the Point

To the Point

A Story about E. B. White

by David R. Collins
illustrations by Amy Johnson

A Carolrhoda Creative Minds Book

Carolrhoda Books, Inc./Minneapolis

To my brother Dick — for too many reasons to share on paper

This book is available in two editions:
Library binding by Carolrhoda Books, Inc.,
  a division of Lerner Publishing Group
Soft cover by First Avenue Editions,
  an imprint of Lerner Publishing Group
241 First Avenue North
Minneapolis, MN 55401 U.S.A.

Website address: www.lernerbooks.com

Library of Congress Cataloging-in-Publication Data

Collins, David R.
   To the point : a story about E.B. White / by David R. Collins; illustrations by Amy Johnson.
       p.   cm. — (A Carolrhoda creative minds biography)
   Summary: Follows the life of the popular author of essays, poems, and children's books, from his childhood in rural New York State to his death at the age of eighty-six.
   ISBN 0-87614-345-1 (lib. bdg. : alk. paper)
   ISBN 0-87614-508-X (pbk. : alk. paper)
   1. White, E. B. (Elwyn Brooks), 1899–1985—Biography—Juvenile literature. 2. Authors, American—20th century—Biography—Juvenile literature. [1. White E. B. (Elwyn Brooks), 1899–1985. 2. Authors, American.] I. Johnson, Amy, ill. II. Title. III. Series.
PS3545.H5187Z6   1989
818'.5209—dc19   88-27418

Manufactured in the United States of America
9 10 11 12 13 14 – MA – 07 06 05 04 03 02

Table of Contents

Chapter One

Silently En slipped inside his brother's room. He listened. There was no sound. Everyone in the house was downstairs.

There it was, sitting on the desk. En hurried to the chair. He slid a piece of paper into the new machine. His hands fell to the keys. He pressed one letter at a time:

```
Elwyn Brooks White
```

—and smiled. His name looked so important typed on the paper.

Again he struck the keys, this time faster. Suddenly the keys wouldn't type. "I broke it!" he gasped.

En slipped the paper out of the machine. Now his name did not look very important at all. Picking up a pencil, he printed above his name:

I am sorry I broke your typewriter.

He walked to Stan's bed and set the paper on the pillow. Then he returned to his own room. An hour later Stan White appeared in his kid brother's doorway.

"So you broke my typewriter, En?"

En looked up from his bed. At least Stan had called him by his nickname. If he had been really angry, he would have said, "Elwyn Brooks White, you are in big trouble." Maybe Stan wasn't *too* angry.

"I'm sorry. I just wanted to try it out."

"Well, you didn't break it. You just jammed the keys. When you want to use it, ask me. You're lucky that typewriter is okay."

As Stan left the doorway, En sighed. He did feel lucky.

But Elwyn Brooks White thought he had always

been lucky. From the day he was born—July 11, 1899—his father claimed he was a good-luck baby because he arrived on the eleventh day of the seventh month. Some people thought seven and eleven were lucky numbers.

Samuel White, En's father, had had some luck himself. His piano manufacturing business brought in a handsome income. It allowed his wife, Jessie, to hire servants to care for their house in Mount Vernon, New York. Jessie and Samuel White wanted to enjoy all the time they could with their six children.

Marion, Clara, Albert, Stanley, Lillian—with so many older sisters and brothers, En spent little time alone. Each of them felt quite able to take care of their youngest brother, often fighting for the opportunity.

The White children enjoyed the best of what money could buy. Yet Samuel White had no intention of spoiling any of them. With privileges came responsibility.

At five years old En was offered a dog. Along with the new pet would come the tasks of washing and feeding it and keeping it in-bounds. The dog could run in the yard and the cellar, but the front rooms and kitchen were to be off-limits.

In addition Mr. White could inspect the dog as well as its master at any time. En accepted these conditions.

With his dog, Mac, beside him, En explored. He roamed through the fields of buttercups and flowering dogwood trees, pausing to carefully inspect each gopher hole and jack-in-the-pulpit. He climbed the trees of Wilson's Woods. At Snake Pond he watched the salamanders and frogs. Nature fascinated him. He could not get enough of it.

While En liked the sights of nature, he loved its sounds. At night he listened to the starlings outside his window. They chirped their messages. Crickets and owls joined in. Now and then the muffled blast of a foghorn drifted in from Long Island Sound to accompany the songs of darkness.

One day Samuel White brought home a surprise for his children. He set an incubator and fifty chicken eggs on the back porch. En could not wait for the eggs to hatch.

The exciting day finally arrived. Each chick pipping itself out of its shell brought a new cry from the White children. Eagerly En's brothers and sisters gathered up the trays of new chicks and rushed off to show them to the neighborhood.

But En stayed behind. Three eggs remained. He set them near the stable behind the house. The minutes slipped slowly away. En watched and waited. Then it happened. The shell of one egg cracked open. Then another. Finally the third chick pipped its way clear. En felt like a proud father!

Content with the freedom and fun of life in the big gray house on Summit Avenue, En was not happy to begin school. In his classes he day-dreamed. En pictured himself on skates darting and dashing across Dell Pond while his classmates sang "Winter Joy." As his teacher read about herds of wild horses on the frontier, En thought of the stable at home, with its harnesses and strong smell of hay. History lessons reminded him of his Meccano building set. He had spent hours in his attic putting together the blocks, building bridges and forts.

En dreaded his public-speaking course most of all. He feared being in front of people. At Lincoln School pupils in public-speaking classes were to give one speech before their classmates each term. En was glad they spoke in alphabetical order. Often the term would end before the teacher came to the *W*s.

No one was happier than En when school let out for summer vacation. The summer season had only one drawback: it brought pollen, which hurt En's eyes. To solve his son's allergy problem, Samuel White found a new vacation spot—a cottage on the peaceful shores of Great Pond, one of the Belgrade Lakes in Maine. It was said there was little pollen there.

En loved the new vacation spot. The fresh air, the open sky, the birds and the butterflies, the islands in the lake, the waves' white foam—this was a wonderful world. There was always a new path in the woods to explore, another group of squirrels to watch. Here the White family could relax. They canoed, fished, and swam—no clocks to watch or assignments to hand in. En wandered freely with his brothers and sisters or by himself. Adventure was always just beyond the next tree. The thought of returning to school after that first trip to Maine was only made bearable for En by the promise of the next summer.

As the seasons passed, life slowly changed for Elwyn Brooks White. By the time he was twelve, he was the only one still living at home with his parents. All of his brothers and sisters had gone away for college or had gotten married.

Excited laughter and lively discussions no longer filled the big gray house. The radio was played less and at lower volumes. The wild sounds of shouts thrown from room to room and footsteps rushing up and down the stairs had ceased.

Samuel and Jessie White found the new peacefulness restful. They seemed content to be by themselves. But to En the calm was suffocating. Often he felt not just alone, but lonely.

Chapter Two

About this time, when he was eleven or twelve, En made an unusual friend. The huge dictionary in his brother Albert's room was old and ragged. En had watched his brothers and sisters use the book often, yet he was not really familiar with it. Now that there was no one in the house to play games with, En investigated the dictionary.

"Become a word collector," Samuel White often advised his children. "It is a happy person who can use words correctly."

15

En found his father's advice was true. The dictionary contained just the right words for his school reports and stories. Before long En found he enjoyed reading the dictionary to amuse himself. He felt like Columbus. He kept a daily journal, marking his discoveries. En tried to find the perfect words to recreate events, to capture his exact feelings about them. The right combination of words was like the music of his father's finest piano. It could express the beauty of a sunset, the fury of a storm.

"There is a kind of magic in words," En wrote in his journal. "I do not know what the future holds for me, and yet I know that words will play a part in it."

In 1911 Elwyn Brooks White took his writing into a new world, a world outside his home and school. A popular magazine for young readers, *St. Nicholas Magazine*, offered a silver badge for anyone sending in a story worthy of publication. En sent in his manuscript about walking in the woods in wintertime. The editors liked the story, and "A Winter Walk" appeared in the June issue. En was thrilled.

"Now I am truly a writer," he wrote in his journal. He was twelve years old.

En now welcomed the time alone—he needed it to write! Words were his friends, and they gave him a new power. Animals sprang to life on the pages he wrote: a mouse, a dog, a herd of cows. He could recreate fun times with his brothers and sisters in a story or poem. When his mother read the essay he wrote about her garden, her eyes filled with tears. His description of summertime at Great Pond, complete with illustrations, made his father grin. And the fantasy he created about a mighty hero with the initials E. B. W. helped him overcome his fear of speaking in front of his classmates.

Yes, words strung together were like a necklace. They could be pulled tight and tense, like tough leather. Or they could hang heavy and loose with colorful beads. With the right words to describe them, one's thoughts could be whirled and twirled, flapped and snapped.

Not that En spent *all* his time writing. Too many things interested him for that. In winter he could be found skating—creaking and cracking over the ice as he played goalie in neighborhood hockey games. And he loved riding his bike. Few others could manage the wild acrobatics he could, sitting backward on the handlebars.

And at home, when he wasn't tackling a story on Stanley's typewriter, En was playing the piano.

"Well done!" his parents would exclaim. But En knew he wouldn't become a professional pianist.

As he grew into his teens, En thought more and more about his future. He felt at ease with boys—but girls almost made him panic. He graduated from Mount Vernon High School in 1917 without ever having a date. Would he ever marry? he wondered. What kind of job would he find? How easily his older brothers and sisters seemed to make decisions. En worried about making a wrong choice, taking a wrong direction. He did not want to make any mistakes.

In 1917 America entered World War I. En was scheduled to enter Cornell College in the fall. But many of his friends were enlisting for military service. Should he? He loved America; he was certain of that. Yet the thought of killing other human beings—no, that thought sickened him. If only someone could tell him what to do, he thought.

"My birthday!" En wrote in his journal on July 11, 1917. "Eighteen and still no future! I'd be more contented in prison, for at least I would know precisely what I had to look forward to."

Caught up in the patriotic fever sweeping the country, En visited the local army center in Mount Vernon and took a physical exam. Even if he had definitely wanted to join the army, he could not. He did not weigh enough. So that summer En became a Farm Cadet on Long Island, helping other boys harvest the crops of American farmers who had gone to fight in the war. But he also found time to visit Great Pond for a few weeks.

En arrived at Cornell College in the fall of 1917. By scoring high on his entrance tests, En won a six-hundred-dollar scholarship. He decided to sign up for the college newspaper staff in addition to his courses so he could continue with his writing. Since many of the staff members belonged to Phi Gamma Delta, a fraternity at Cornell, En joined it too. Although writing was something one did alone, it was fun to share thoughts and ideas with other writers.

"Just keep the grades up," his father wrote. "Don't spend all your time writing for the newspaper."

En paid little attention. The life of a reporter was exciting. He loved seeing his name in print with the news stories he wrote. His friends liked working with him and respected the way he used words. They nicknamed him "Andy," after the president of Cornell, Andrew A. White.

It took a "D" grade in an English class to shake En up. Never had he received such a low mark in his favorite subject. Words were his special world, language his love.

En tried to find excuses for his low grade. He imagined he had an illness. His body was thin—he was wasting away! And then there was the war. If he were a soldier, he could just think about fighting. As it was, his thoughts were divided. While he sat in his classrooms, he thought about many of his friends and classmates who were risking their lives in the war. Why, it seemed almost unpatriotic to get good grades!

The school year ended six weeks early so students could work in the factories that produced war materials. Hoping to enjoy a more cheerful summer, En went to work for his father at the piano factory. He bought a used convertible and dated often, trying to overcome his shyness around girls. It was a fun summer! En *almost* managed to forget the war.

But as he thought about going back to college for his second year, En felt ashamed. Young men, including some of his friends, were still fighting.

Some had died. Others had been spending their time working *hard* in college. En had not been doing either.

It was a changed Elwyn Brooks White who returned to Cornell in the fall of 1918. He was ready to accept responsibility. On September 2 he was one of three million American men to register for the draft. Each would be required to become a soldier if his number was selected.

"I'm sure I would not be the best soldier in the world," En wrote in a letter to his father. "But if I am needed, I am ready to go. If I am not needed in the war, I will do my best here."

There was little need to draft students at American colleges and universities. Counting those who registered in September, almost 24,000,000 men were eligible for the draft. Only 2,800,000 were needed to maintain American forces.

En wanted to be ready, though, in case he were called into service. At Cornell he enlisted in the Student Army Training Corps. The training included courses in "War Aims," military law, and drill. He looked like a scarecrow in his oversized uniform. Since many newspaper staff members were away fighting, no newspaper was published that year. En used the extra time to study.

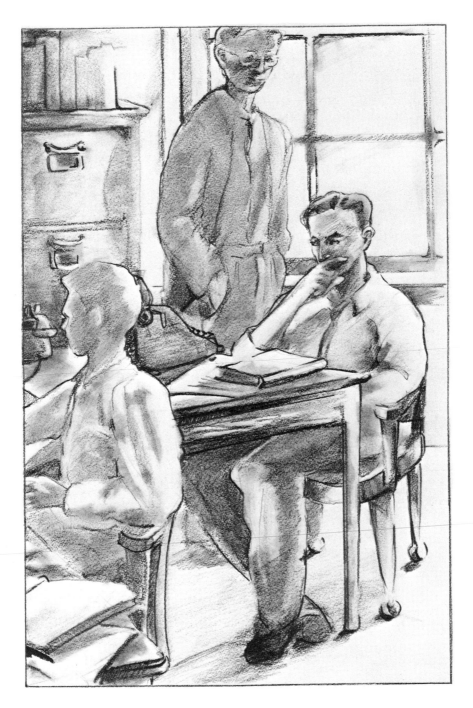

In November an armistice, or truce, was signed that ended the war. En turned in his uniform. As soon as enough staff members returned, the *Cornell Daily Sun* was printing newspapers again. Its office became En's second home. News stories, reviews, features, and poems all rolled from his typewriter. He was back in his world of words.

During his junior year En was picked to head the *Daily Sun* staff, and his fraternity elected him their president. Never had En felt so important. People were reading his words and discussing his thoughts. He had friends who respected him. Yet he was sure that there was a lot about writing that he did not know. Now more than ever before he longed to write with force and clarity. Fortunately three Cornell teachers were ready to help Elwyn Brooks White do exactly that.

Chapter Three

En sat taking notes in his English VIII class. A man with steel-rimmed glasses stood at the front of the room.

"Keep your writing simple," said Professor William Strunk, Jr. "Each sentence you write is like a boat. One extra word can sink it."

Not only did En write down his teacher's words, but he thought about their meaning. As a word lover, En knew how to let words flow onto paper. He was sure he often used too many. After listening to Professor Strunk, En began working to make his writing clear and "clean"—free of unnecessary words.

Professor Martin Sampson challenged En to think about what he was writing. As a college senior, En knew he had a tendency to take life seriously—maybe *too* seriously. He worried about everything, from whether his hair was carefully parted to what he would do with his life.

"We need more humor in our world," said Professor Sampson. "People don't laugh enough. A writer who brings a chuckle to the reader is a messenger from God."

Humor! Yes, En knew the beauty in laughter. He remembered how his father and mother had smiled at his early efforts to write funny stories. Now Cornell classmates laughed aloud at his witty essays and humorous tales. Language could bring joy, and En was grateful to Professor Sampson for reminding him.

Finally there was Professor Bristow Adams. His literature and writing classes gave En a new idea of what great writers can achieve. Not only were class sessions exciting, but the kind professor also invited students to meet at his home. They came and read their manuscripts aloud, afterward sharing their comments. Mrs. Adams joined the group too, treating En like a son. En soon found himself feeling at home.

Professors Strunk, Sampson, Adams—each fine teacher offered important writing tips and support to his students. Each influenced Elwyn Brooks White in a special way at a time when he was listening carefully. He worked hard to apply their advice to his writing.

En gave advice too. As editor of the *Cornell Daily Sun*, he worked with student reporters every day. The *Daily Sun* was one of two college newspapers in the United States that published an issue a day. It was also the daily paper of Ithaca, New York. En had to make sure each issue was interesting to readers of all ages. Hour after hour he struggled to make each of his sentences, and the paper as a whole, just right.

In 1921 Cornell University graduated Elwyn Brooks White. Now, as he looked toward the future, he was sure he wanted to be a writer. He did not know what kind of writer, or where. But he did know it was time to cast off the nicknames of childhood and college. No longer would he be "En" or "Andy." From now on he would be E. B. White.

E. B. White accepted a job as a reporter for United Press, working in New York City. He soon discovered his decision was a mistake.

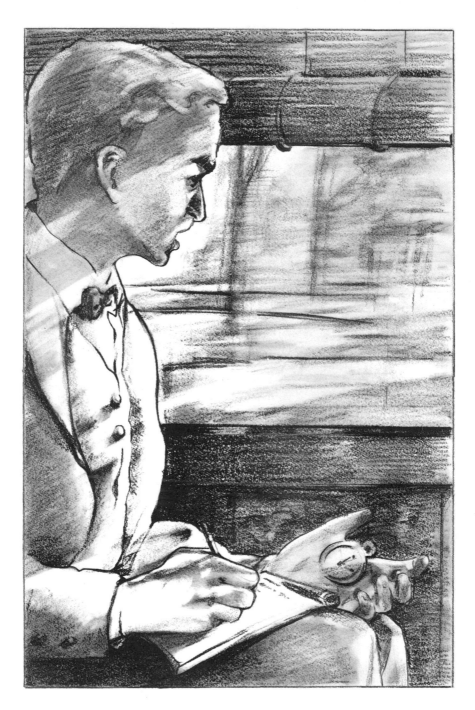

Gone was the friendly teamwork he had enjoyed while working with his friends on the *Cornell Daily Sun*. One day, sent to report on the funeral of a politician, he took the wrong train and missed the event. His editor told him a good reporter was never careless. "Maybe you should get away from writing for a while," the editor continued. "See the country. Then you'll be ready to settle down a bit."

The idea made sense to White. He bought a Model T car and named it Hotspur. Of his automobile he wrote, "It sprang cheerfully towards any stretch of wasteland whether there was a noticeable road underfoot or not. It had clearance, it had guts, and it enjoyed wonderful health."

With a friend from college, E. B. jumped in his Model T and headed west. The two travelers had little money. They went hungry much of the time and camped on the hard ground.

The six-month trip left White with even less money and a renewed desire to get back to writing. In the fall of 1922 he took a job with the *Seattle Times* newspaper. The editor let him have his own column of poems and essays. But within a year several staff members were let go. E. B. was among them. Sadly he headed back east.

While staying with his parents in Mount Vernon, White again began searching for a job in New York City. An advertising agency hired him, but it wasn't what he really wanted. It didn't allow him to express his thoughts and feelings.

"Every word is aimed at selling a product," he complained to his father. "There's no chance to create a mood or build from one's own imagination."

"Then find a job where you can do those things," Samuel White replied.

E. B. wasn't sure where that would be so he continued in his routine, hoping something would come along. When three Phi Gamma Delta fraternity friends from Cornell asked him to room with them in New York City, En jumped at the chance. Maybe this was the improvement his life needed.

It wasn't enough. To escape his depression, White spent his savings on a one-seat, twenty-foot catboat. With it he often sailed around the north shore of Long Island.

One morning he pulled his boat onto a beach and went swimming. When he returned, a man with a rifle stood beside his catboat.

"Who are you? What do you want?" the stranger demanded.

E. B. sputtered, his words catching in his throat. Clearly no answer would satisfy the man.

"This beach belongs to J. P. Morgan. It is not open to the likes of you," the stranger growled.

E. B. wanted to argue. Yet something about the rifle stopped him. Seconds later he guided his catboat away from the shore.

That night White could not get to sleep. He was angry. This country welcomes people from countries far away, yet some Americans won't welcome their peaceful neighbors. It was something to think about. Why, it was something to write about too! E. B. rolled and tossed in bed. Thoughts popped into his mind; his fingers tingled to write them down. He wanted to use writing to change things in the world, to make them better. Suddenly he sat up in bed. "I don't just want to be a writer!" he said aloud. "I've *got* to be a writer!"

Chapter Four

His decision to devote himself to writing and finding a job to suit his talents gave E. B. White fresh energy and enthusiasm. Since returning to New York, he had occasionally sent manuscripts to local magazine editors. Some had been published. But White wanted to be a professional writer whose words and thoughts appeared regularly to a reading audience.

The Conning Tower had used a few of his poems, but White knew the chances of finding full-time work with a small literary journal were slim.

34

On February 19, 1925, E.B. bought the first issue of a new magazine called *The New Yorker.* As he studied its pages, White knew this was his kind of magazine. *The New Yorker* covered New York City life in a light and witty personal style. It captured the heartbeat of the biggest city in America with poems, essays, stories, and articles. Quickly E. B. put together some selections of his work and sent them off to Harold Ross, the editor.

In April *The New Yorker* published the first of E. B. White's articles. Filled with the quick-paced, clever style E. B. had perfected in advertising, the article described the arrival of spring. It was clearly the right type of material for the magazine. Within weeks his second essay appeared—a humorous article entitled "Defense of the Bronx River." Then came a cheerful tale called "Child's Play," which recalled the time when a waitress had spilled buttermilk on his best suit.

Yes, Harold Ross seemed to like White's writing. He even invited E. B. to stop by the offices of the magazine. But would Ross offer him a full-time job? Armed with courage and more manuscripts, E. B. went to meet him.

It was a tense and exciting morning for White.

He was greeted by an assistant editor of *The New Yorker,* Katharine Angell, who praised his work. Equally generous with compliments was Harold Ross. White left the office with a firm job offer.

Yet again E.B. struggled with the decision. He liked the people he would be working with, and *The New Yorker* would give him countless writing opportunities. But he did not like working in an office and under deadlines. Fortunately Ross understood.

"Whenever you want to come and work for us," the editor said, "you can do so."

At this same time a friend coaxed White into taking a trip to Europe. It would be free, he said, if E.B. would write a movie script about the journey. E.B. agreed, and off they went. The two-month trip gave White a chance to think about the rare writing opportunity the new magazine could give him. After returning he eagerly accepted Harold Ross's offer at *The New Yorker.*

Although E.B. White had thought he would not like working in an office, he soon found he had been wrong. Ross let White write as he pleased, and Katharine Angell offered cheerful conversation as well as skillful editing. He also discovered a good friend in another *New Yorker* writer named James Thurber.

By 1926 magazine readers could recognize the White style even though his essays were not signed. His writing was crisp, clever, and familiar. So often his clumsiness, forgetfulness, or carelessness had gotten him into trouble, and now E. B. could write freely about them. Readers loved his humor and could relate to his experiences.

Readers of *The New Yorker* also found that E. B. White could be serious. He wrote about problems that people faced every day. He suggested ways of improving city and national government.

"I read every word this White fellow writes," declared New York Mayor Jimmy Walker. It was said that President Calvin Coolidge did too.

White liked writing for *The New Yorker*. But during the next few years, he began to realize it was not just the magazine he enjoyed.

Katharine Angell had become more than just an editor to him—she was the most important woman in his life. She was always willing to listen, always trying to help. Their friendship grew into love. E. B. and Katharine were married in November of 1929.

That same year a collection of E. B. White's poems, entitled *The Lady is Cold,* was published. The book won praise from reviewers for its "honesty" and "warmth." Next came a book he wrote with James Thurber. Although White did not intend to stop writing for *The New Yorker*, he knew he wanted the chance to write more books. Books last longer than magazines, and White enjoyed giving them to his friends.

When the Great Depression hit, White's articles in *The New Yorker* expressed sadness and understanding. He knew what it felt like to be out of work. With banks failing and workers losing their jobs, he cheered people up with descriptions of foolish moments in his life—his clumsy efforts to make money and be successful. If ever the country needed E. B. White's humor, it was now.

"Thanks for giving us a smile once a week," wrote one reader. "It's about the only thing we can afford."

December 21, 1930, was a day that made E. B. and Katharine smile. They became parents. They named their son Joel McCoun White.

E. B.'s feelings about being a father slipped into his writing. "Parenthood consists of being enthused, confused and amused," he wrote. "I think I will spend most of my time in the middle stage."

As White wrote to his readers, they also wrote to him. Each day brought another stack of letters. E. B. enjoyed that special friendship that grows between writers and their audiences through the thoughts and feelings words express.

Most of *The New Yorker* focused on local activities, but White wrote about events around the country and the world. To help unemployed people during the Depression, E. B. promoted the idea of the government helping make work for them. "Men and women need jobs," he wrote, "and our nation's leaders who have vision and compassion will answer that need."

In 1933 a Civilian Conservation Corps (the CCC) was started under the new American president, Franklin Delano Roosevelt. People across the country were put to work constructing new buildings and developing land projects. White was delighted with the government program.

As the country changed, E. B. White changed as well. He grew tired of the noise and dirtiness of New York City. Memories of summers in Maine returned. He longed for the open fresh air, walks in the woods, the sounds of nature.

Between 1935 and 1936, both of White's parents died. Though he was thirty-seven, he felt like an orphan. He looked for some way to brighten up his life, some cheerful change.

When a friend heard about a small farm for sale near the coast of Maine, he told E. B. The moment he saw the property, White knew it was what he wanted. Once he and Katharine had bought the forty acres, the farm became a private zoo. Sheep, geese, chickens, pigs, and even a captive mouse joined the White household—or at least the barnyard.

Weekly magazine deadlines became a strain on White. There was always a fence to fix or a room to paint. Although Katharine continued doing editorial work for *The New Yorker* at the farm, E. B. decided to try writing for another magazine. *Harper's* came out monthly; by writing for it, E. B. would have more time for farm work. He would still be able to write about what interested him, and he would finally be able to sign his name to his essays. *Harper's* also reached many of the same readers as did *The New Yorker*.

White's first *Harper's* column appeared in late 1938 under the title "One Man's Meat."

E. B. shared his opinions about the day's news events. In the columns that followed, he expressed his concerns about the military buildup of Germany and the danger of war. Sadly, many of his predictions came true, and in late 1941 America plunged into World War II.

War brought unhappy changes to families across the country. E. B. White wrote to comfort and encourage them. He shared stories about his son's experiences attending a one-room country schoolhouse. He wrote about the farm and jobs that needed doing but never got done. He welcomed readers into his life through the pages of *Harper's*. They learned how his family rationed food and clothing. In big cities and on small farms, Americans found a friend in E. B. White. His words gave them hope, made them think, and helped them laugh and cry.

Now the monthly deadlines no longer satisified White. He had too much he wanted to say. Writing once a week would give him more opportunity to speak out, so he rejoined *The New Yorker* staff in 1943. Harold Ross was glad to welcome him back.

About this time an unusual fellow began to

pop up again in E. B.'s thoughts. Stuart Little was a well-dressed mouse-child who had first appeared in a dream to White. Whenever a niece or nephew had asked for a story, E. B. had created another tale about the brave and cheerful Stuart. Joel had enjoyed the stories as well. Maybe other children would like reading about the mischievous mouse, he now thought.

Another door was opening for Elwyn Brooks White. How strange that holding the door open was a red-capped, smiling mouse!

Chapter Five

E. B. White's first book for children, *Stuart Little*, was published in 1945. The story of a two-inch mouse born to human parents, Mr. and Mrs. Frederick C. Little, brought giggles and glee to boys and girls. Stuart gets locked in a refrigerator, is tossed in a garbage truck, and drives his own car.

"Stuart Little is a lot better than Mickey Mouse," wrote one reader. "We love him!"

Not everyone agreed. Some adults did not like the thought of a baby mouse being born to human beings! Even Harold Ross thought Stuart should have been adopted.

E. B. White simply shook his head. "I followed my instincts in writing about Stuart," White explained, "and following one's instincts seemed to be the way a writer should operate."

Stuart Little quickly won fans—fifty thousand copies sold in a month. It was clear that White's words had touched the hearts and minds of young readers. They could easily cross the fence that separates reality from make-believe.

E. B. White, though, had no intention of giving up writing for adults. He rented an apartment in New York City to work in when he wasn't in Maine. He continued to write about animals on the farm in many poems and essays. City-dwellers came to know the country life that E. B. loved. In his clear, uncluttered writing, they could smell the hay, hear the cows, and see the barn.

One truth about farming bothered E. B. Farmers who raised fowl and livestock usually liked their animals, and yet these peaceful creatures met tragic ends. Pigs, White thought, were the saddest victims of all because people often laughed at them. Once plump, the pigs were butchered to make ham, bacon, and pork chops.

E. B. knew there was nothing he could do to change the situation in real life. But on paper anything could happen!

White made something happen—something special. From his typewriter came a story about an eight-year-old girl named Fern. Her barnyard adventures with a chubby pig named Wilbur and a big gray spider named Charlotte A. Cavatica were published in 1952.

"There's not much in the book *Charlotte's Web*," wrote one reviewer. "Only love, death, courage, hate, beauty, friendship, fear, revenge—just everything in life."

Yet it was not praise from reviewers that White wanted. He hoped to please young readers. When letters started pouring in at the rate of two hundred a week, E. B. breathed easier. The boys and girls liked *Charlotte's Web*. That was what mattered.

"I loved your book about Charlotte," wrote one girl in Illinois. "I hope I can be as good a friend as she was."

"No one writes like you do," another fan wrote. "But why does it take you so long between books?"

E. B. White chuckled at the letters from his young friends. Few of them knew he had written and was still writing books for adults.

Most of his works were essays and poems for *The New Yorker*.

In 1957 E. B. White gave up his New York apartment. He finally decided he wanted to spend all his time on the farm. He could mail his writing to publishers from anywhere, but he could only enjoy his barnyard family by being with them.

When a college friend sent E. B. a copy of the booklet they had used in Professor Strunk's classes at Cornell, it brought back memories. It also gave White an idea. He had learned so much about rules for good writing from his late teacher—rules that helped him make a living. He wanted to show others, as his teacher had, how to write crisply and clearly; so E. B. took the booklet, carefully updated it, and added a few tips of his own. It was published in 1959. This book, *Elements of Style* by Strunk and White, quickly became a bestseller.

For years E. B. had urged Katharine to give up her editing duties at *The New Yorker*. Both of them were now in their sixties, and E. B. was sure she would enjoy the farm more if she were not working. In 1961 she agreed and turned her full attention to growing plants and flowers. But she always remained willing to read E. B.'s work.

As he neared seventy, E. B. wanted to write another story for children. This time he created a trumpeter swan named Louis, who is born without a voice. The story—of a boy who befriends Louis, a father who is determined to get his son a trumpet, and a female swan who loves Louis—became the book *The Trumpet of the Swan*. It was published in 1970 to the delight of millions of readers.

While the number of E. B. White's literary works continued to grow, so did the number of his awards: a Gold Medal of the American Academy of Arts and Sciences, the Presidential Medal of Freedom, the Laura Ingalls Wilder Award, as well as college and university honorary degrees.

"I've been a lucky man," White told a newspaper reporter in 1976. "I have much to smile about."

In July of 1977 Katharine White died of heart failure. In deep sadness E. B. planted an oak tree that would live on at her gravesite in Maine. Later he published a collection of her essays about gardening.

As best he could, E. B. White continued to write after his wife's death. Visits from his son and five grandchildren lifted his spirits, as did friends who came to chat. He still enjoyed sailing and canoeing.

On November 1, 1985, E. B. White died at the age of eighty-six.

"He made us laugh and he made us cry," wrote one newspaper editor, "and we are the richer for it."

The man who had stirred the hearts and minds of so many readers wrote an even finer tribute—intending it for someone else. As Wilbur the pig sadly mourns the death of his spider friend Charlotte in *Charlotte's Web,* he says, "It is not often that someone comes along who is a true friend and a good writer."

The same could be said of E. B. White.

AFTERWORD

The Writing of *Charlotte's Web*

From the moment *Charlotte's Web* appeared in 1952, it became an instant bestseller. And it continues to be one—enjoying a place of honor in homes, classrooms, and libraries everywhere.

"It's simply a perfect book," noted Bennett Cerf, a famous publisher. "The characters are believable, the story line is suspenseful and moves swiftly, and the setting offers many surprises."

Most bestsellers have important themes. When asked what the theme of *Charlotte's Web* was, E. B. White simply answered, "that a pig be saved."

Not many great writers would spend their time and talent writing about a pig. E. B. White was different. It troubled him that a pig could be carefully fed and tended all summer—then be butchered in the fall. "[People] should be more reliable," White insisted.

Spiders, too, fascinated the author. "Most are harmless," White explained, "but they all carry such mean reputations. They are really skillful, amusing, and useful."

These feelings and fascinations gave birth to *Charlotte's Web*. Wilbur, the pig, and Charlotte, the spider, spin the story while Fern, the young girl, listens and reacts to the events taking place.

Was it easy to write *Charlotte's Web*?

"Writing has never come easy to me," E. B. White said often. "All I have to do is one English sentence, and I fly into a thousand pieces."

Few would guess that a master wordsmith like White would have trouble writing. Yet he was a perfectionist, a writer who wanted every word to be right. He would not settle for less.

E. B. White wrote *Charlotte's Web* inside a small boathouse on his farm in Maine. He had a typewriter, a table, and a wooden bench. Beside the typewriter rested a sketch of the Zukerman barn. "Sketches help me keep the action clear," White explained. Now and then a mouse or squirrel would drop into the boathouse. The author never chased the uninvited visitors away.

When asked why he wrote *Charlotte's Web*, E. B. White smiled. "I really don't know why," he answered. "But I haven't told why I sneeze either. A book is a sneeze."

If the whimsical author is right, *Charlotte's Web* is the most delightful "sneeze" in history!

BOOKLIST

E. B. White's books of fiction for children are available in bookstores and libraries.

Stuart Little. New York and London: Harper & Brothers, 1945.

Charlotte's Web. New York: Harper & Brothers, 1952.

The Trumpet of the Swan. New York: Harper & Row, 1970.

BIBLIOGRAPHY

Commire, Anne., ed. *Something about the Author*, Vol. 2. Detroit: Gale Research, 1971.

Elledge, Scott. *E.B. White: A Biography*. New York: W. W. Norton & Company, Inc., 1984.

Russell, Isabel. *Katharine and E.B. White: An Affectionate Memoir*. New York: W. W. Norton & Company, Inc., 1988.

Sampson, Edward. *E.B. White*. Boston: Twayne Publishers, 1974.

Smaridge, Norah. *Famous Modern Storytellers for Young People*. New York: Dodd, Mead & Company, 1969.